COLORING CHRISTMAS

by Patricia Burke

Cover Art hand drawn
by Doodle Artist Patricia Burke

Cover Art Digitally Colored by Patricia Burke

ISBN: **978-1-951576-05-9**

Patricia Burke would love to see your personally colored version of her art and welcomes you to join and or share them in her Facebook groups.

Find her official fan group here:

https://facebook.com/groups/colormydoodles.patriciaburke/

Or you can share your colored images here:

https://facebook.com/groups.coloringcoop

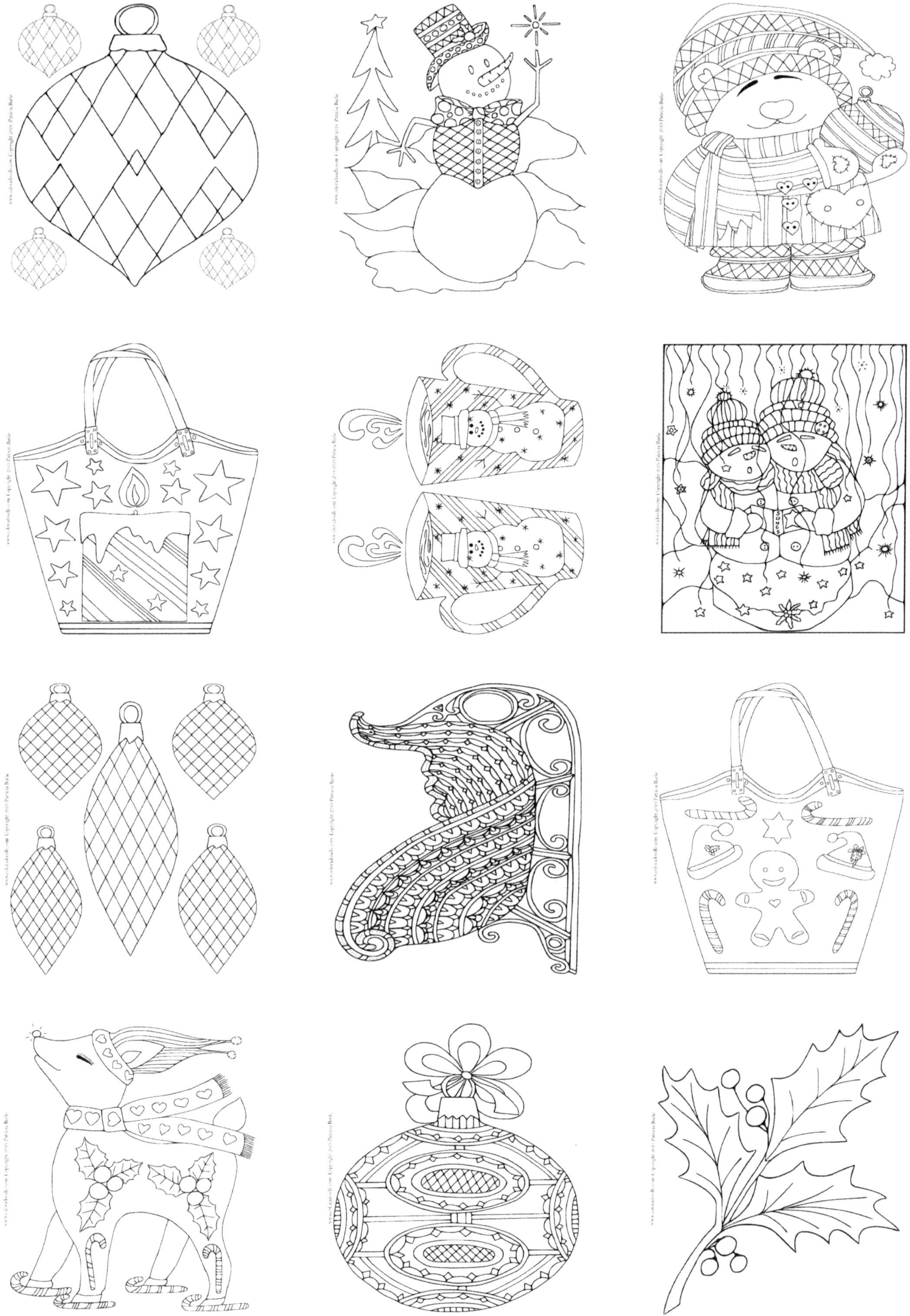

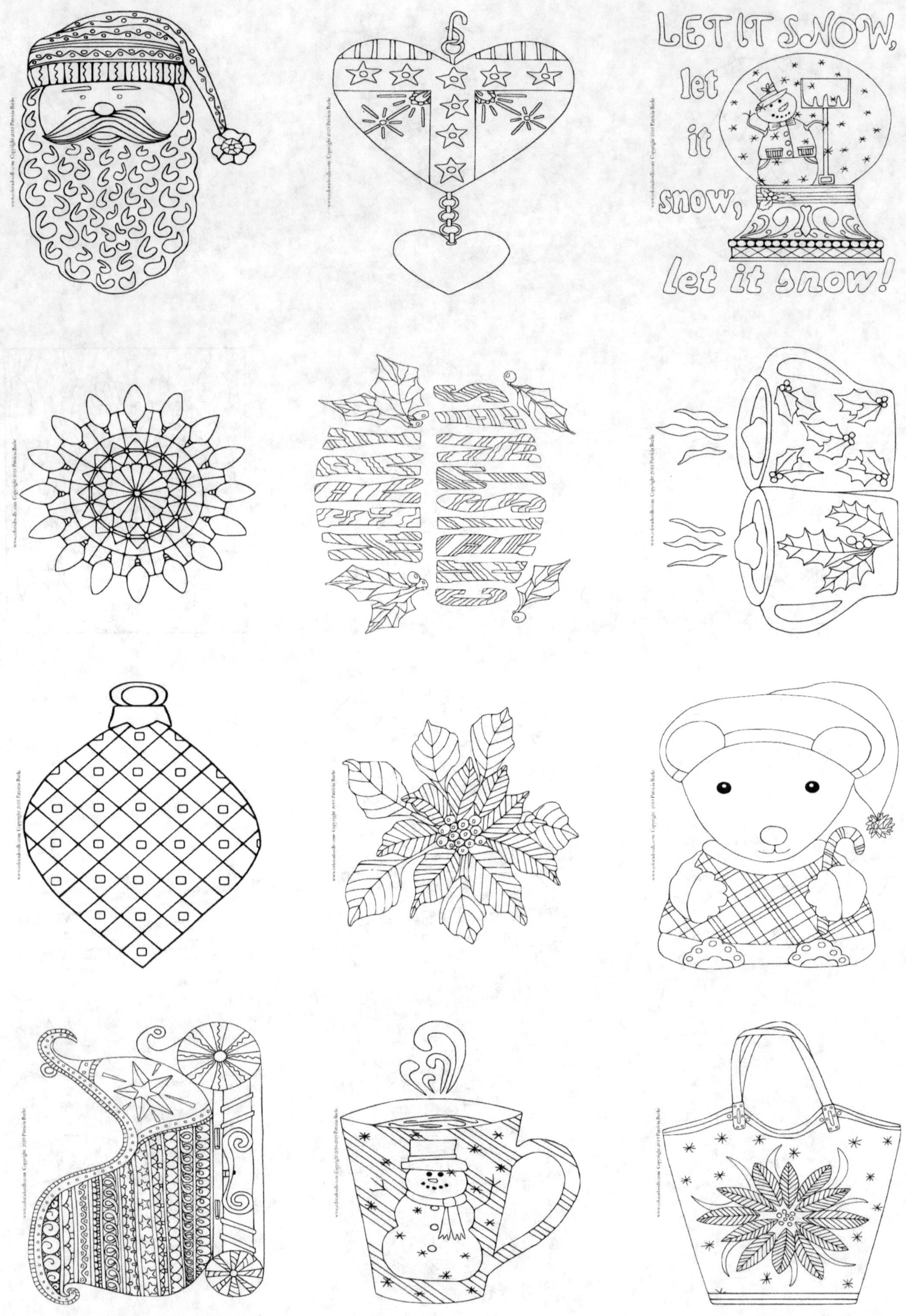
LET IT SNOW,
let
it
snow,
let it snow!

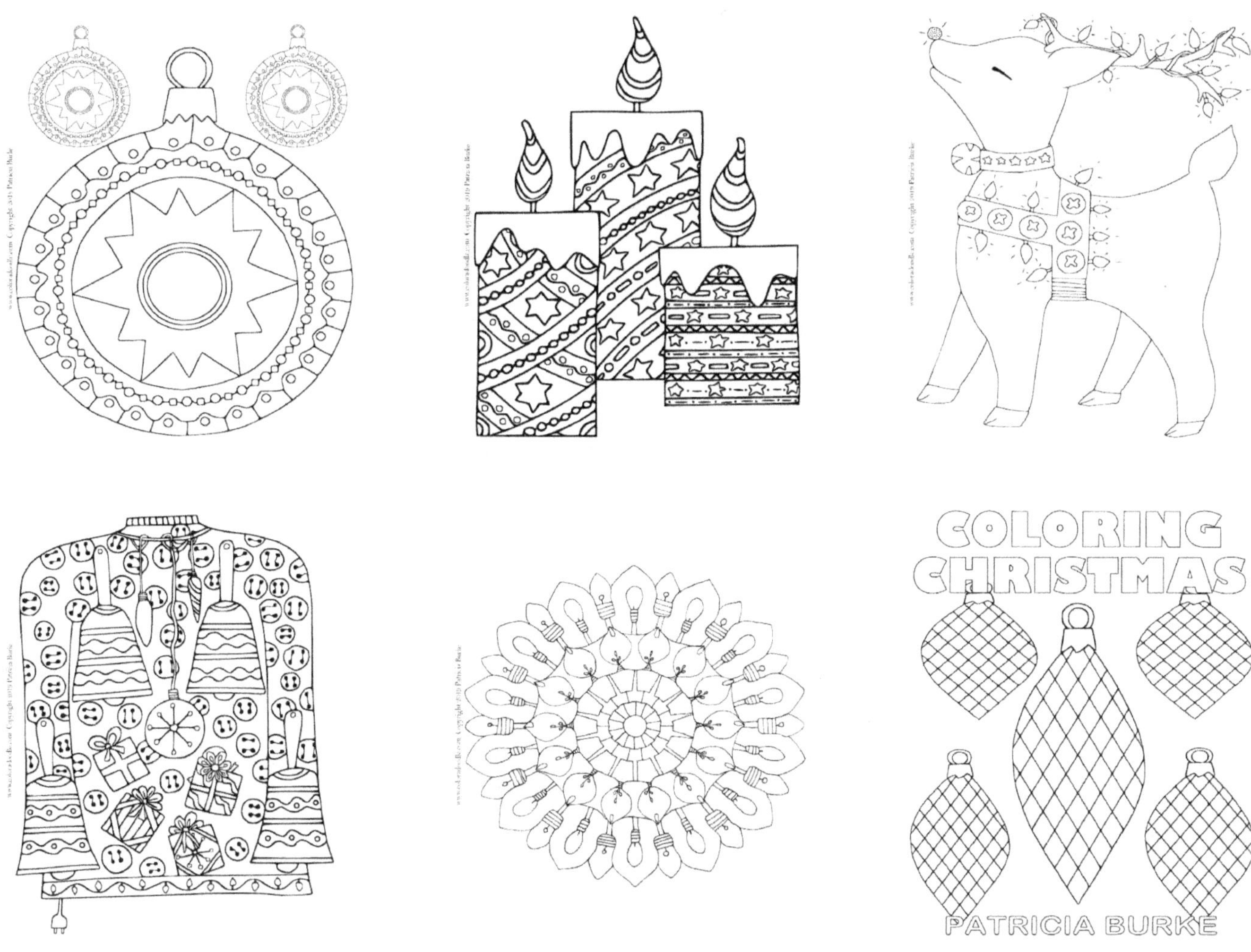

Please consider sharing your enjoyment of my new book.

Go back to the site you purchased this book from,

and leave a short, or long, review.

Thank You

To the members of

~Color My Doodles~

**

You, are the people who make creating fun.

You, are the people who make it easy to be creative.

**

I love what I do and your support allows me to do it.

**

Your membership in my little Facebook group,

means the world to me.

I love seeing what you can do with a blank page that has just

a few semi-organized lines on it.

Your colors inspire me to keep on creating books.

I think of you on those days when

I am struggling for something new to doodle.

**

Thank you so much for sticking with me.

There is a lot more to come...

Happy Coloring!

Thank You

Patricia

~COLORADOODLE COLORING TEAM~

Brenda Hanson

Cari McBroom Jimenez

Charlotte Schroeder Beeston

Debbie West Cummings

Dee Dee Boseman

Jennifer Knisley Preston

Kelly Deuber Taylor

Patricia Jingle

Patty Burke

Susan Nicita

Vicki Ardito

* * * * * *

Follow my artist page on Facebook:

https://www.facebook.com/coloradoodle/

*****

Join my personal group on Facebook here:

https://www.facebook.com/groups/colormydoodles.patriciaburke/

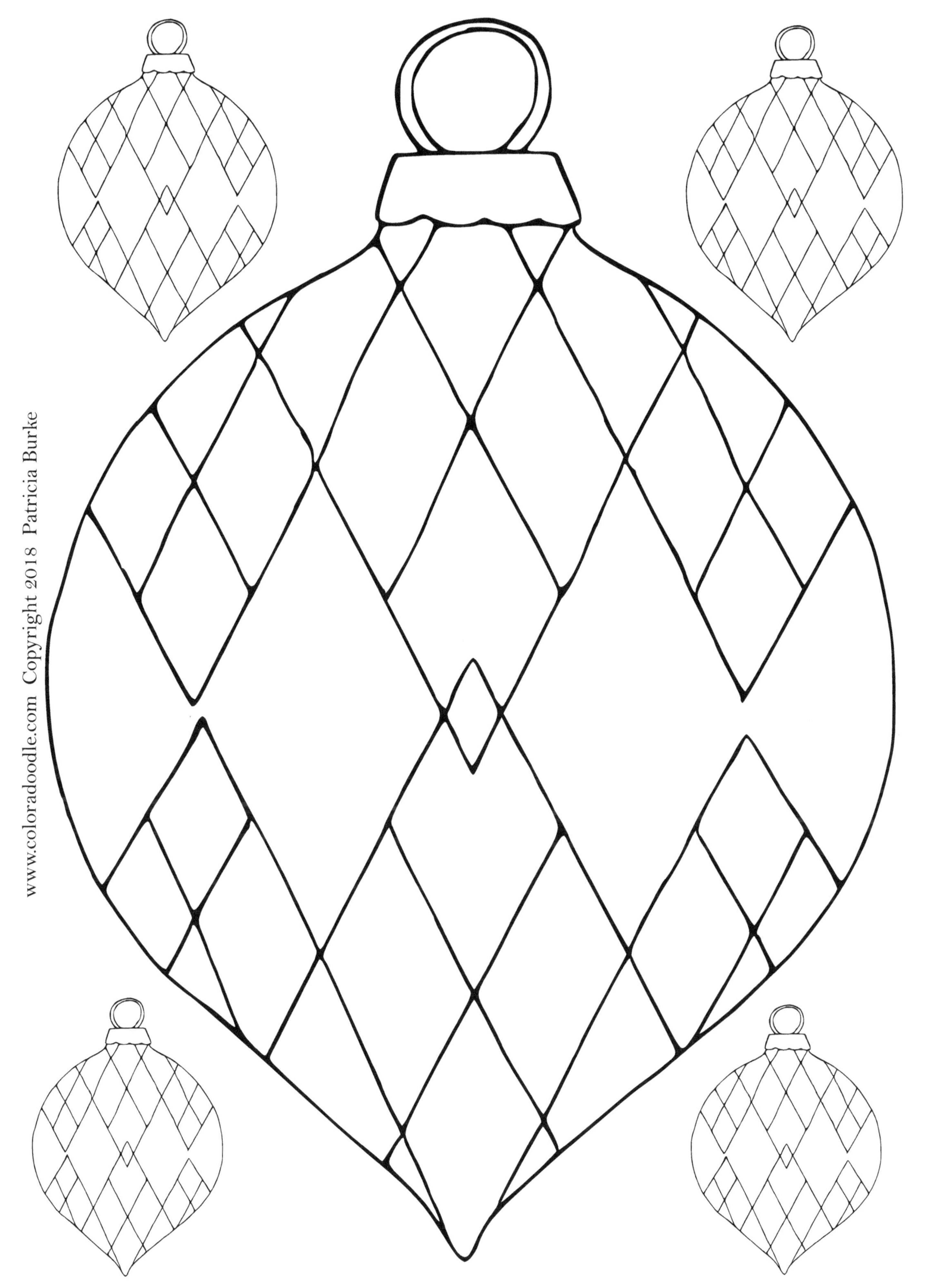

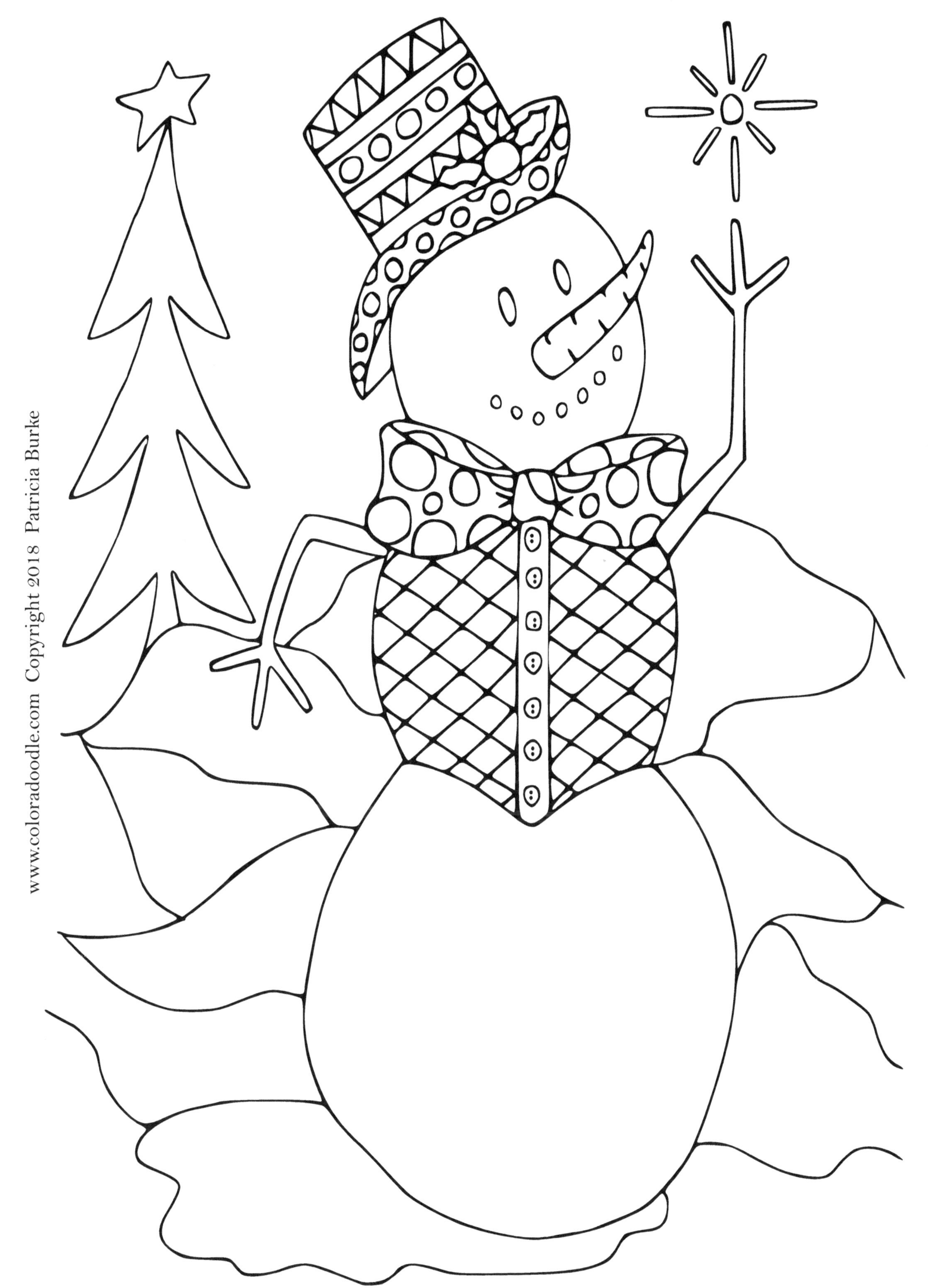

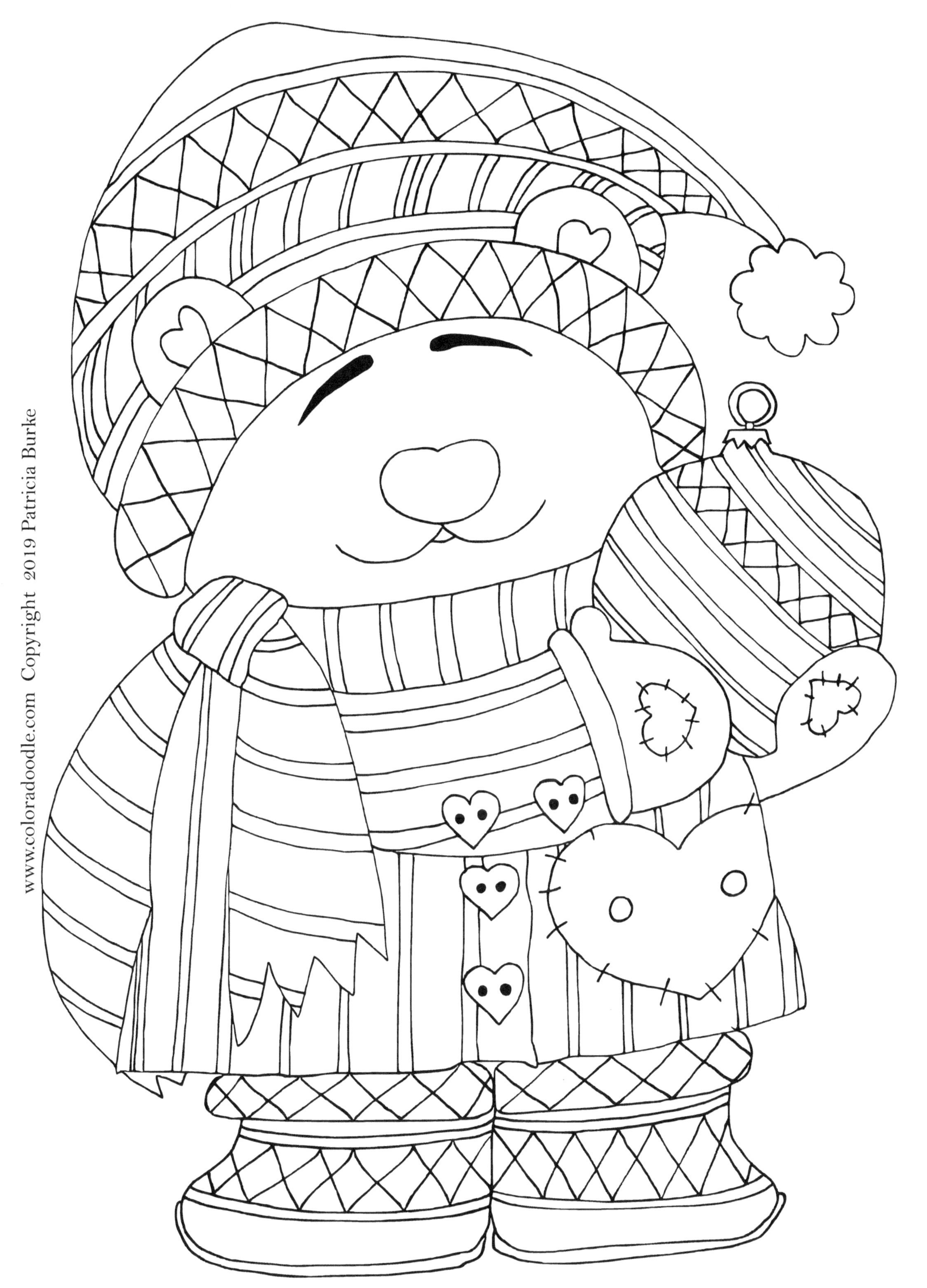

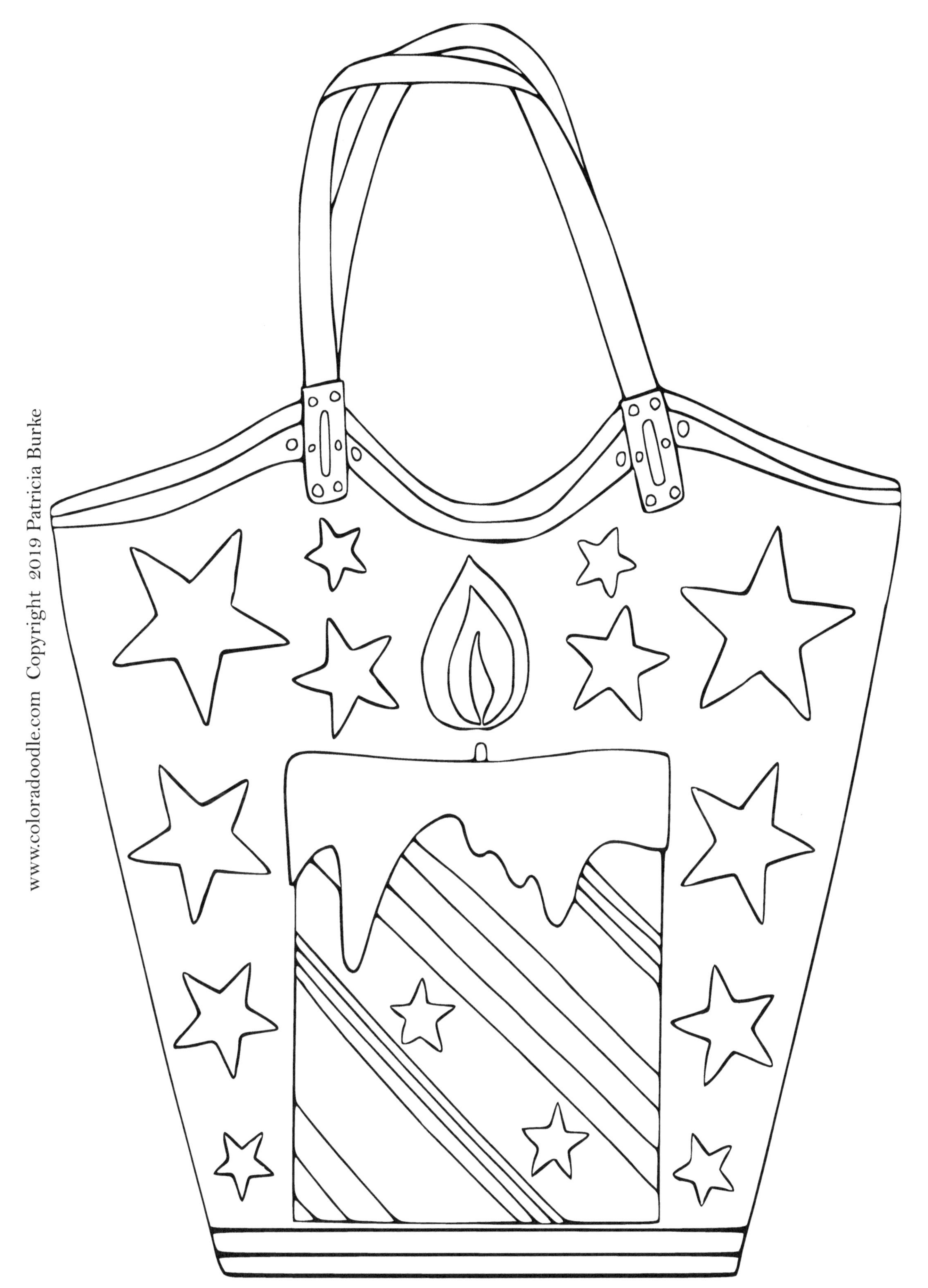

SONGS

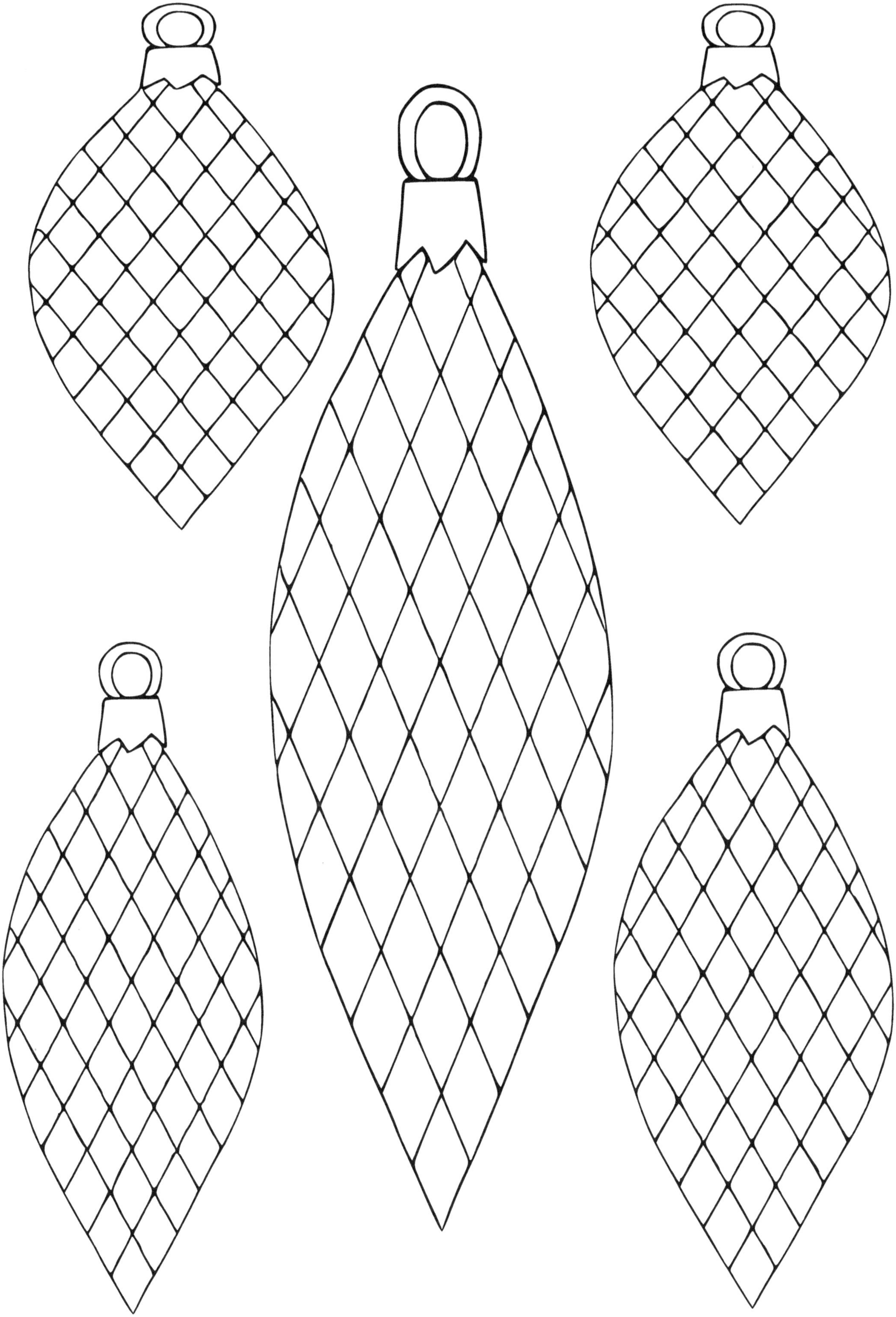

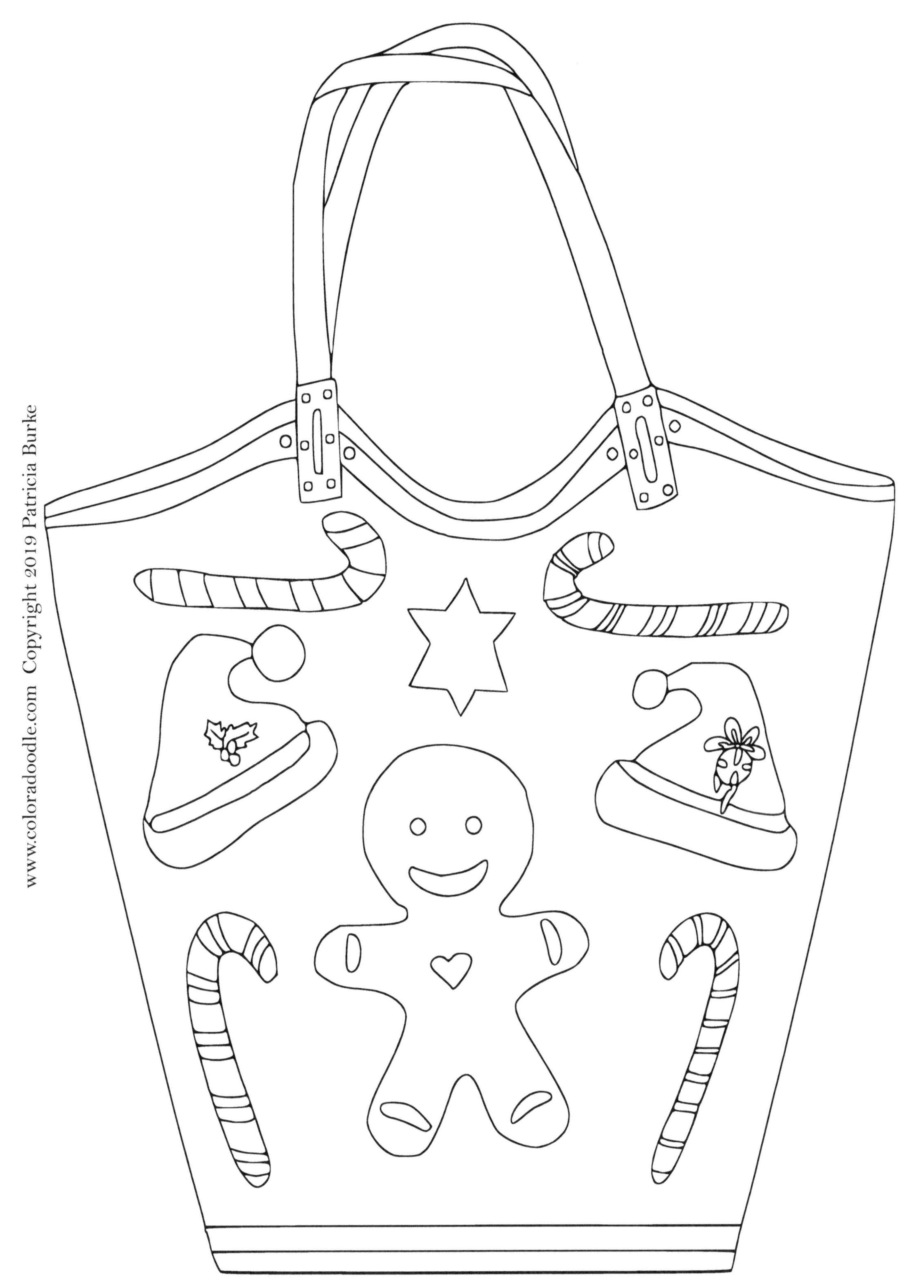

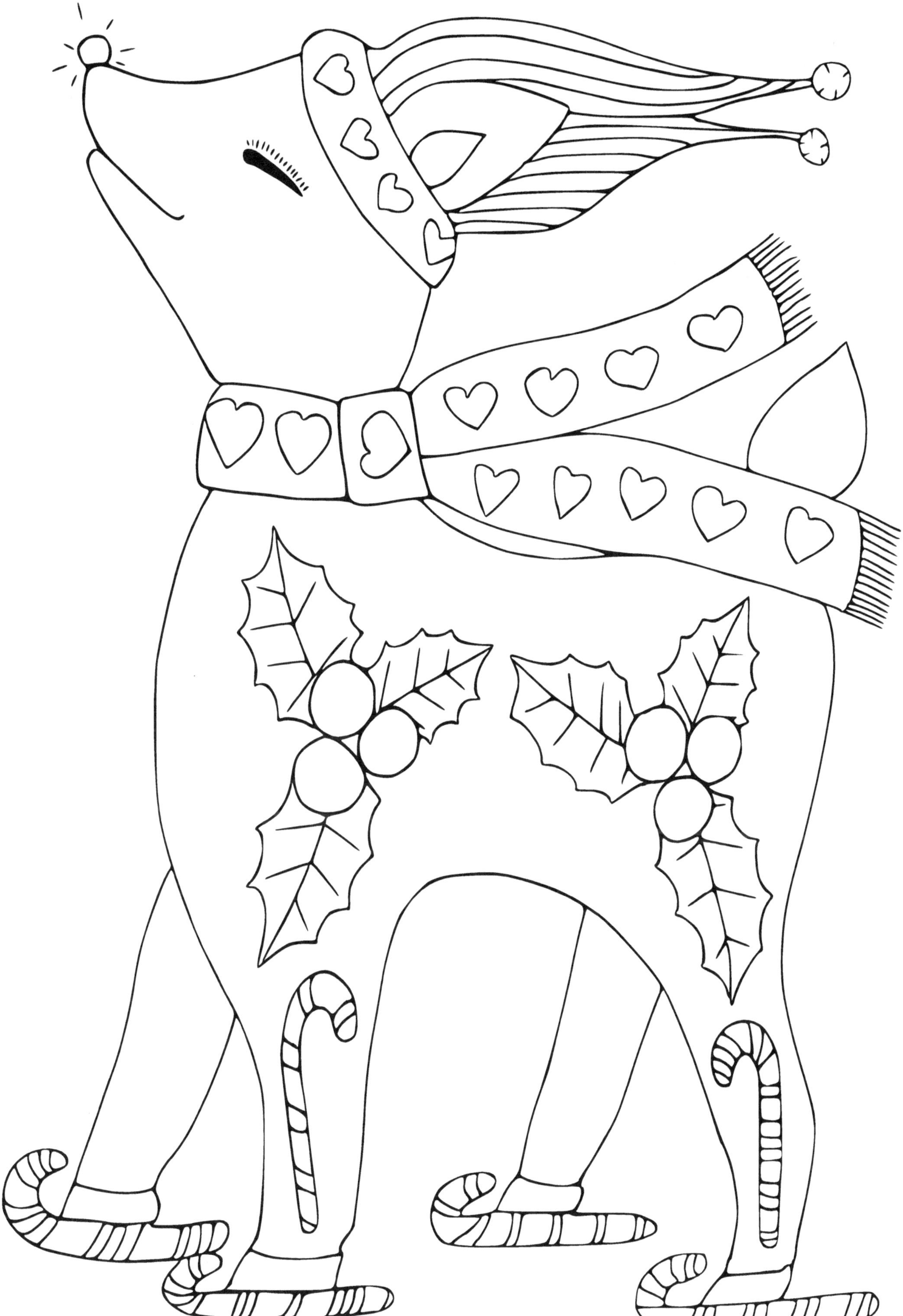

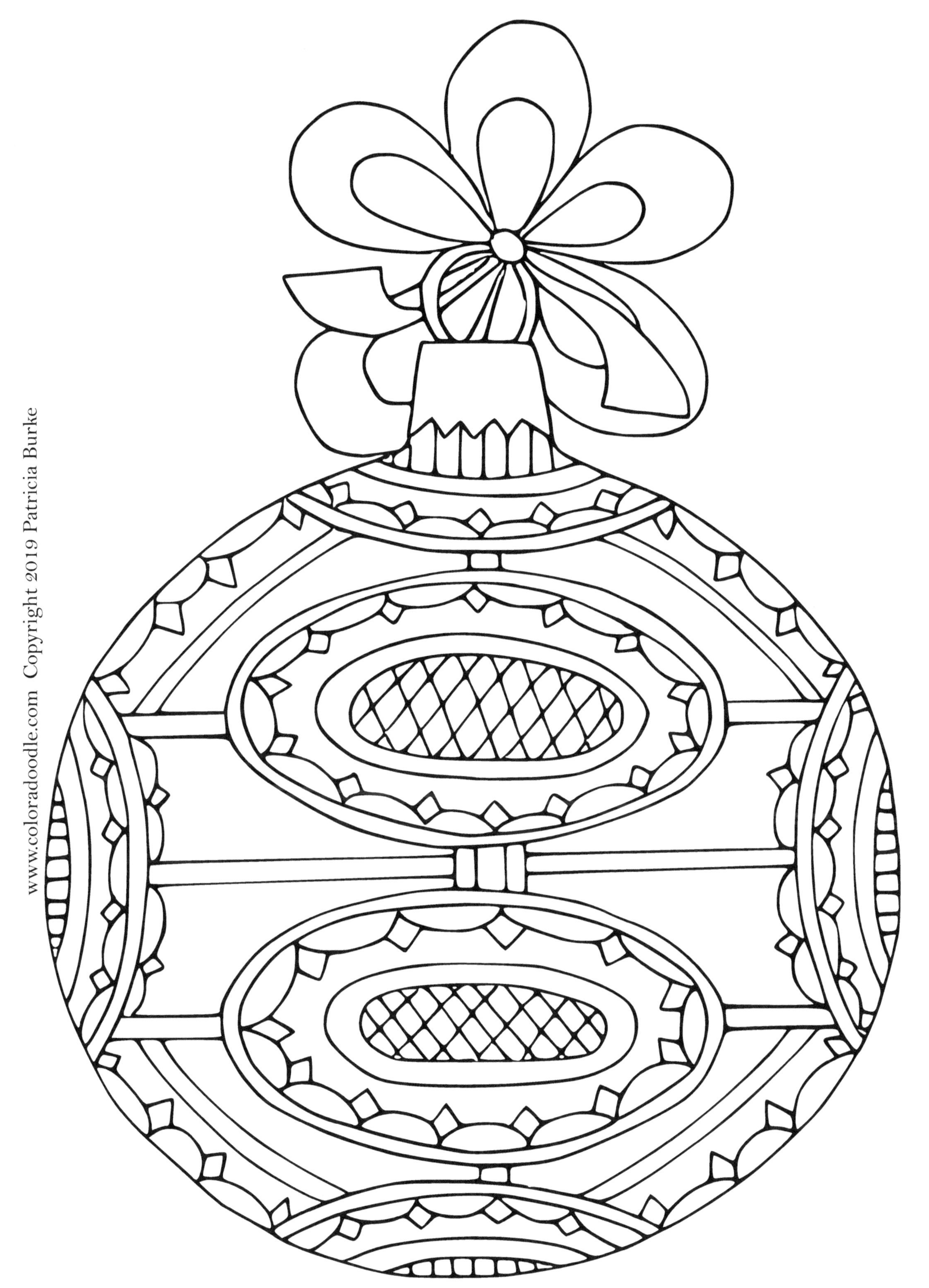

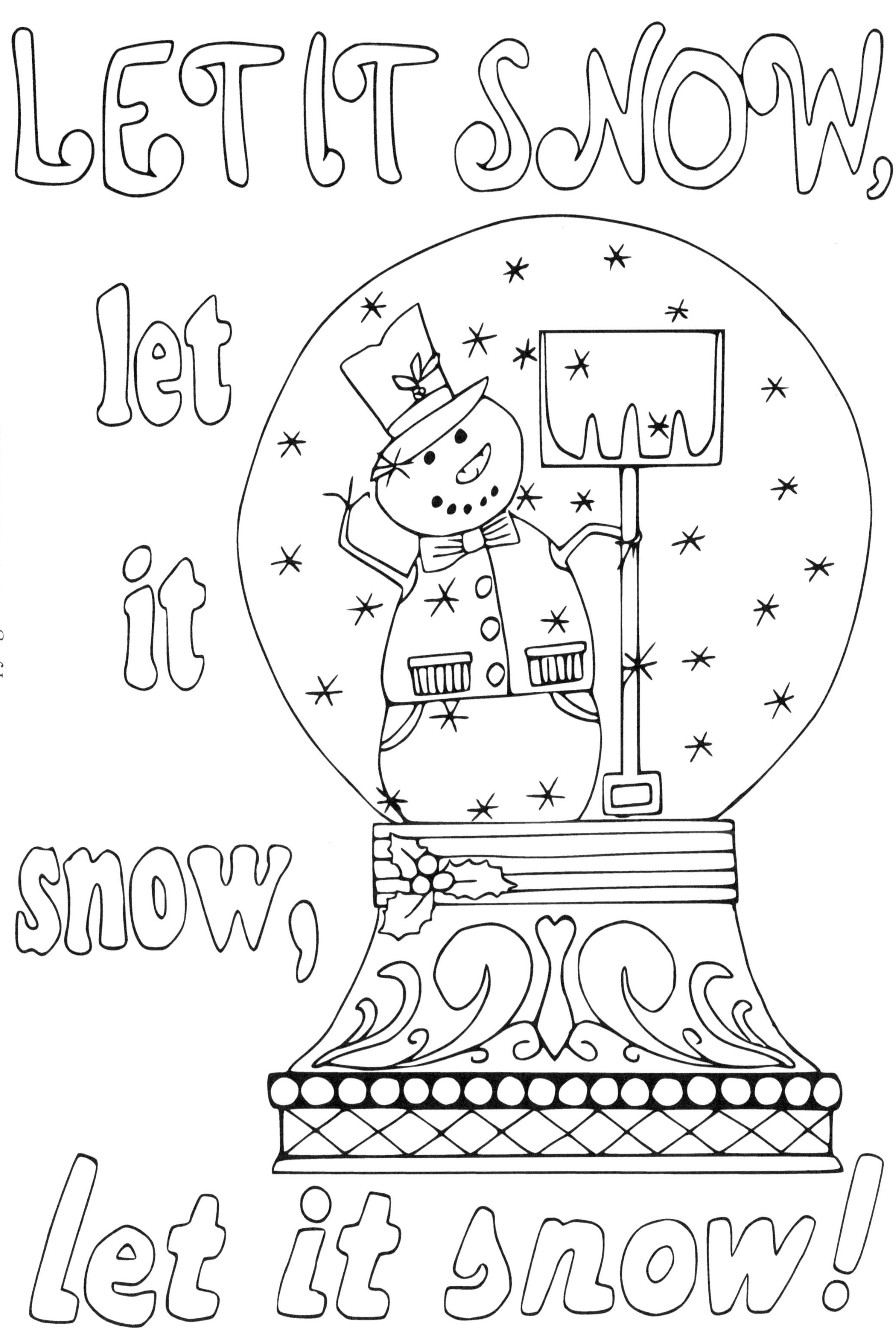
LET IT SNOW,
let
it
snow,
let it snow!

MERRY
CHRISTMAS

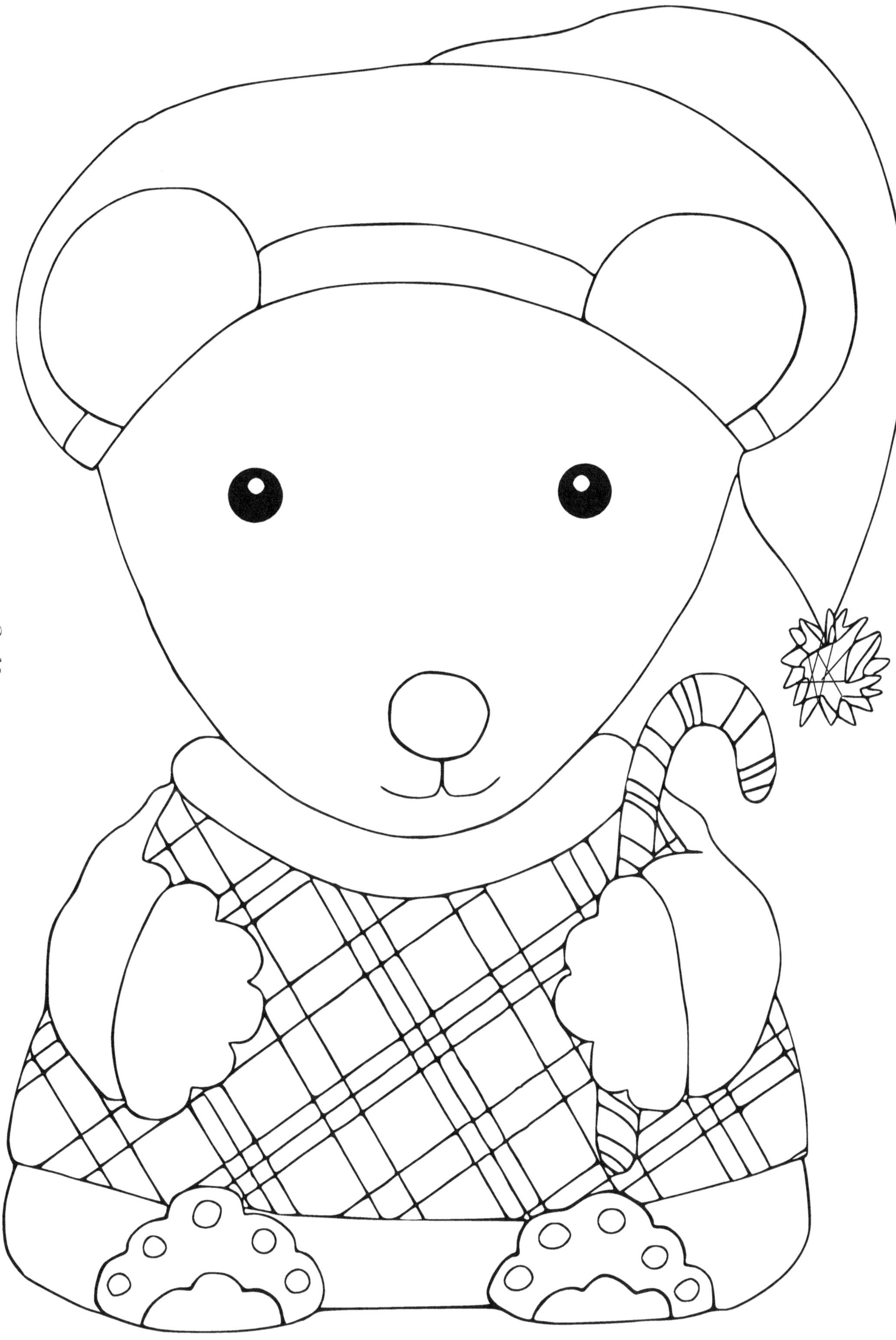

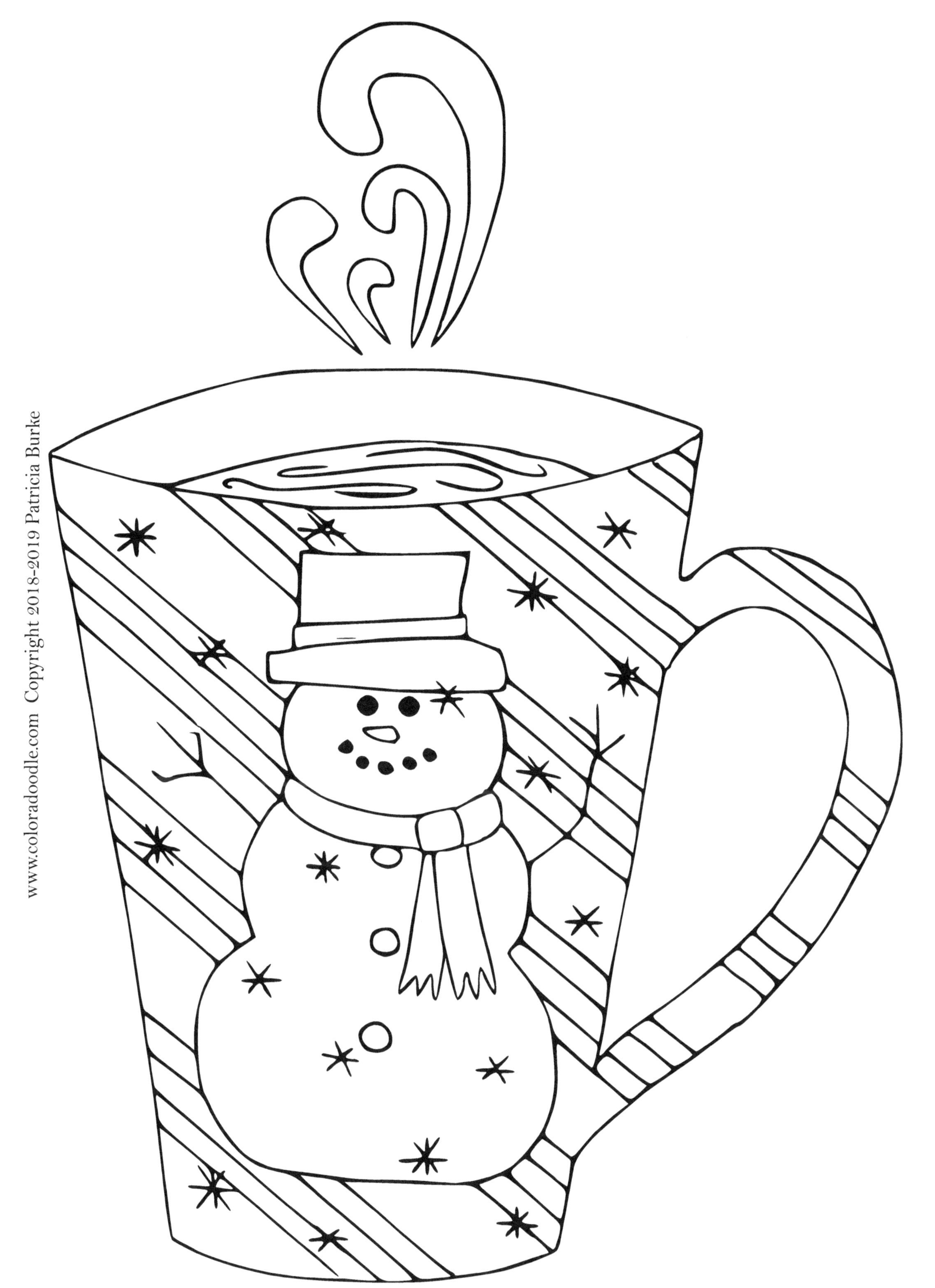

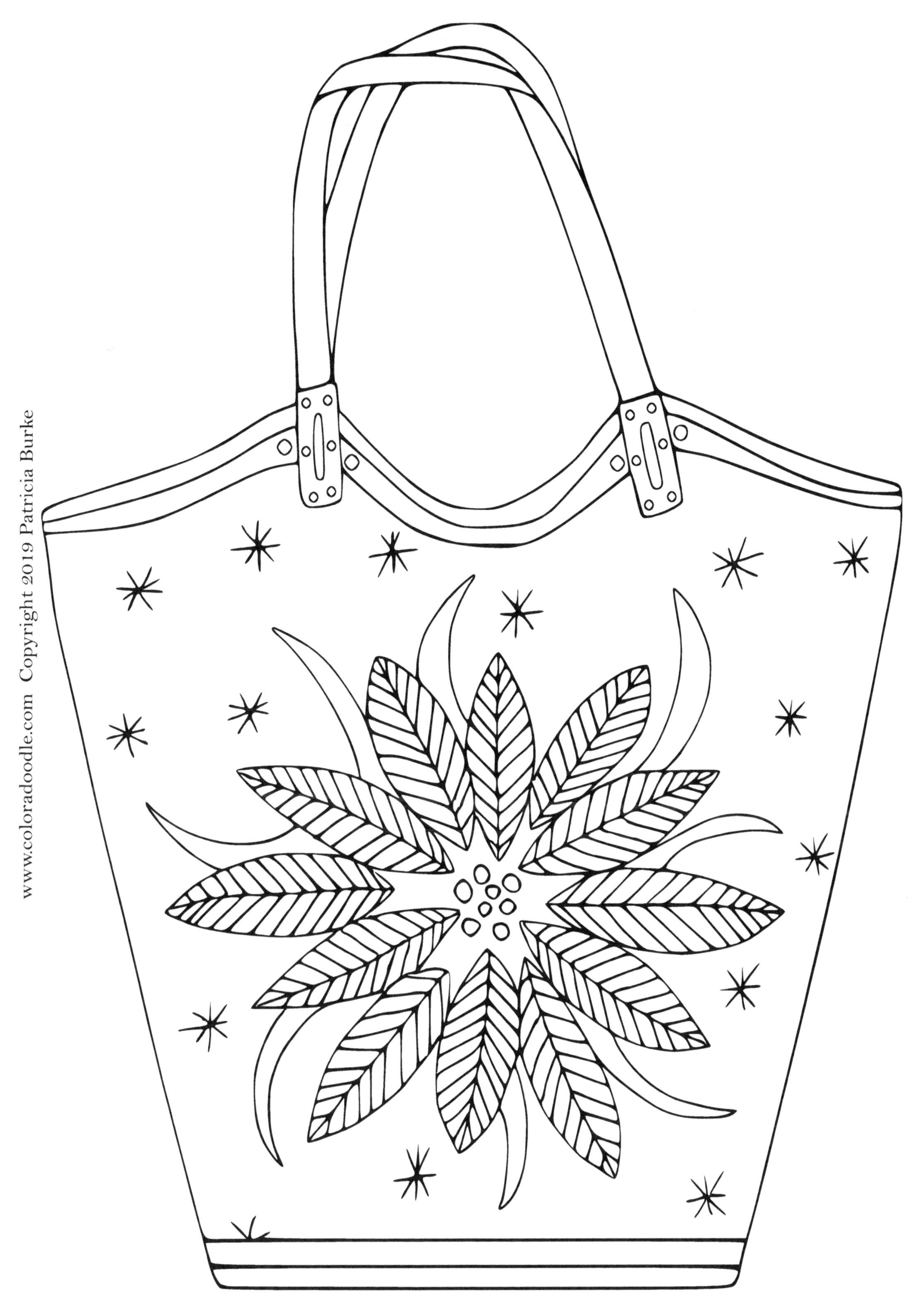

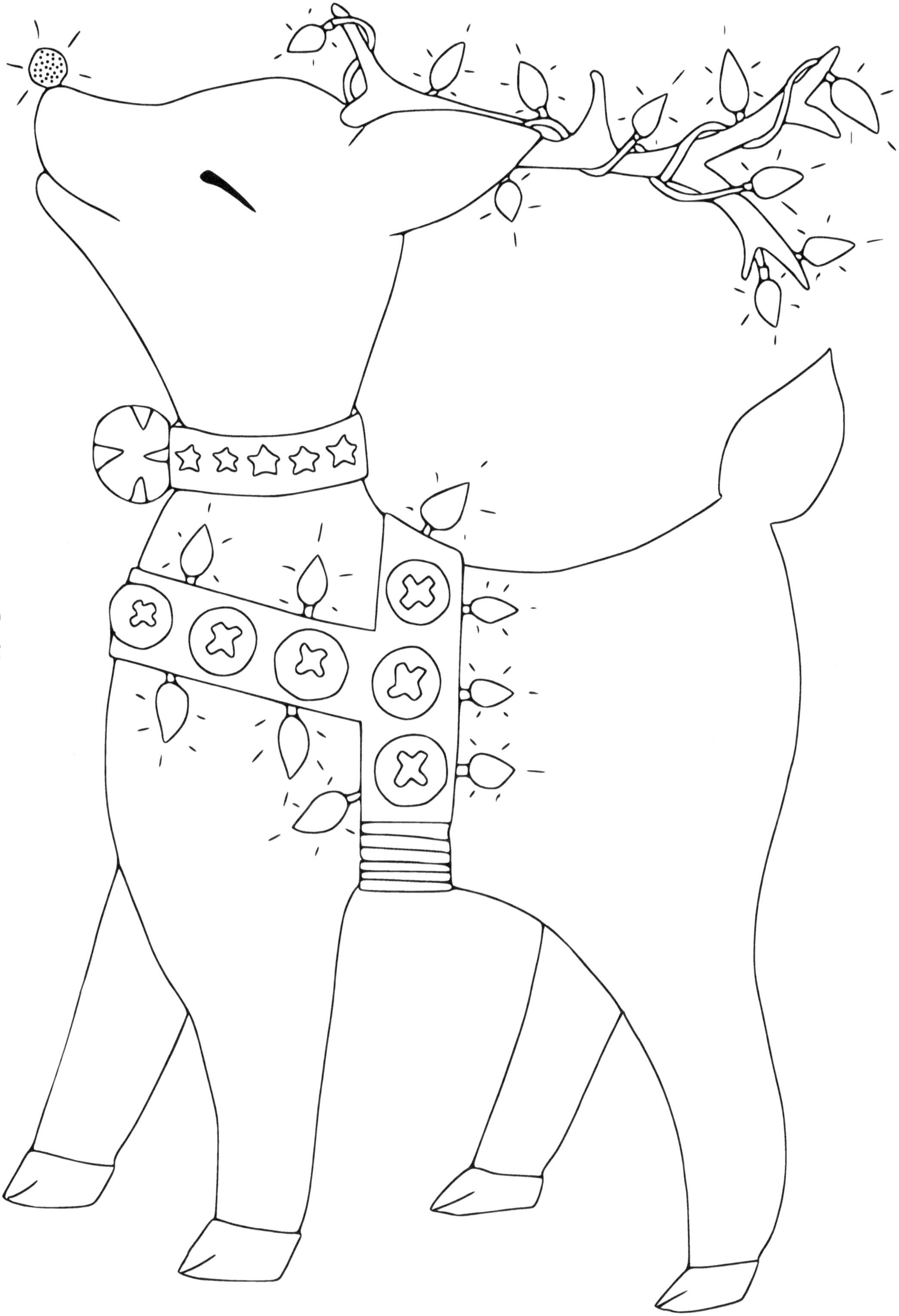

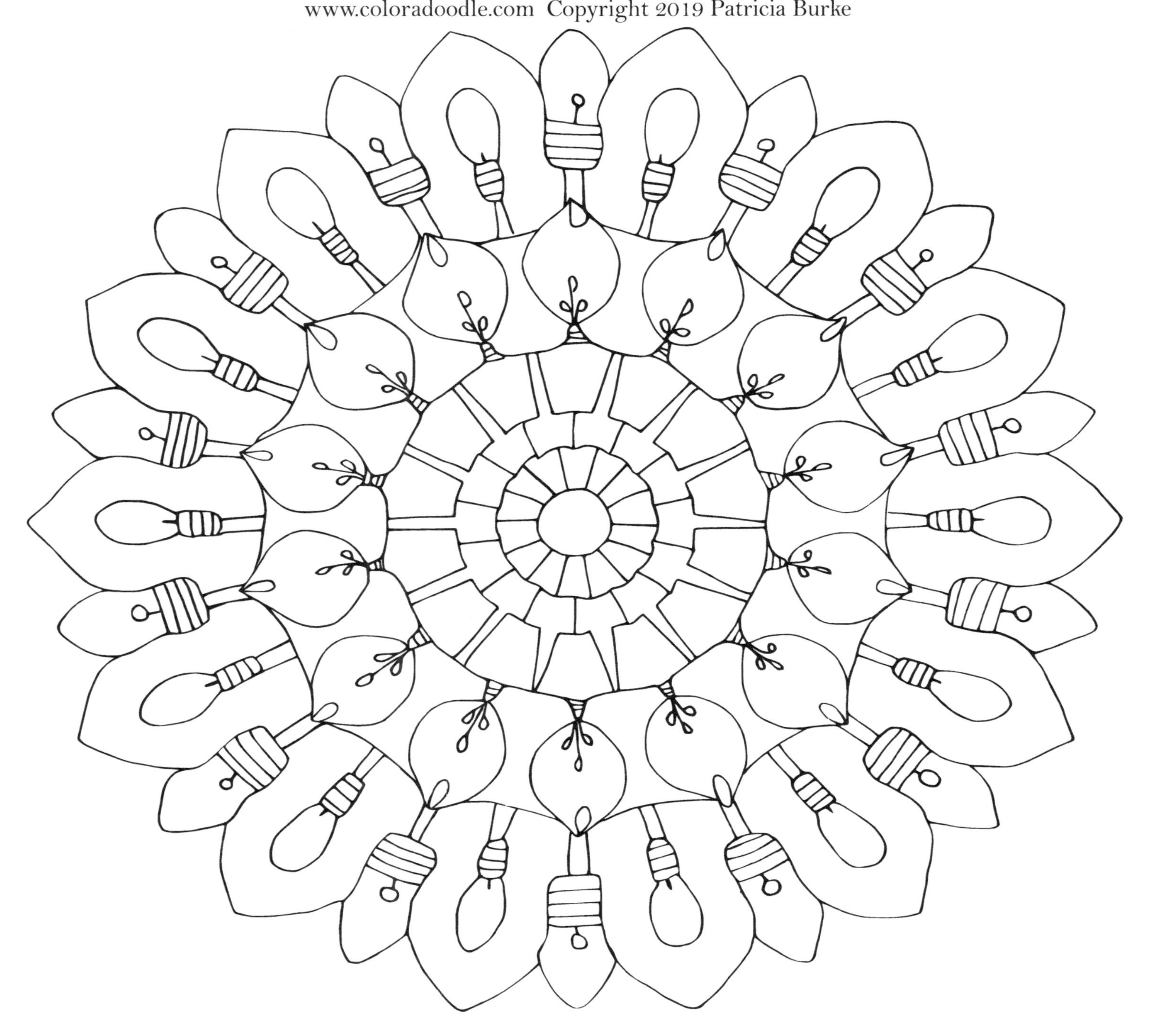

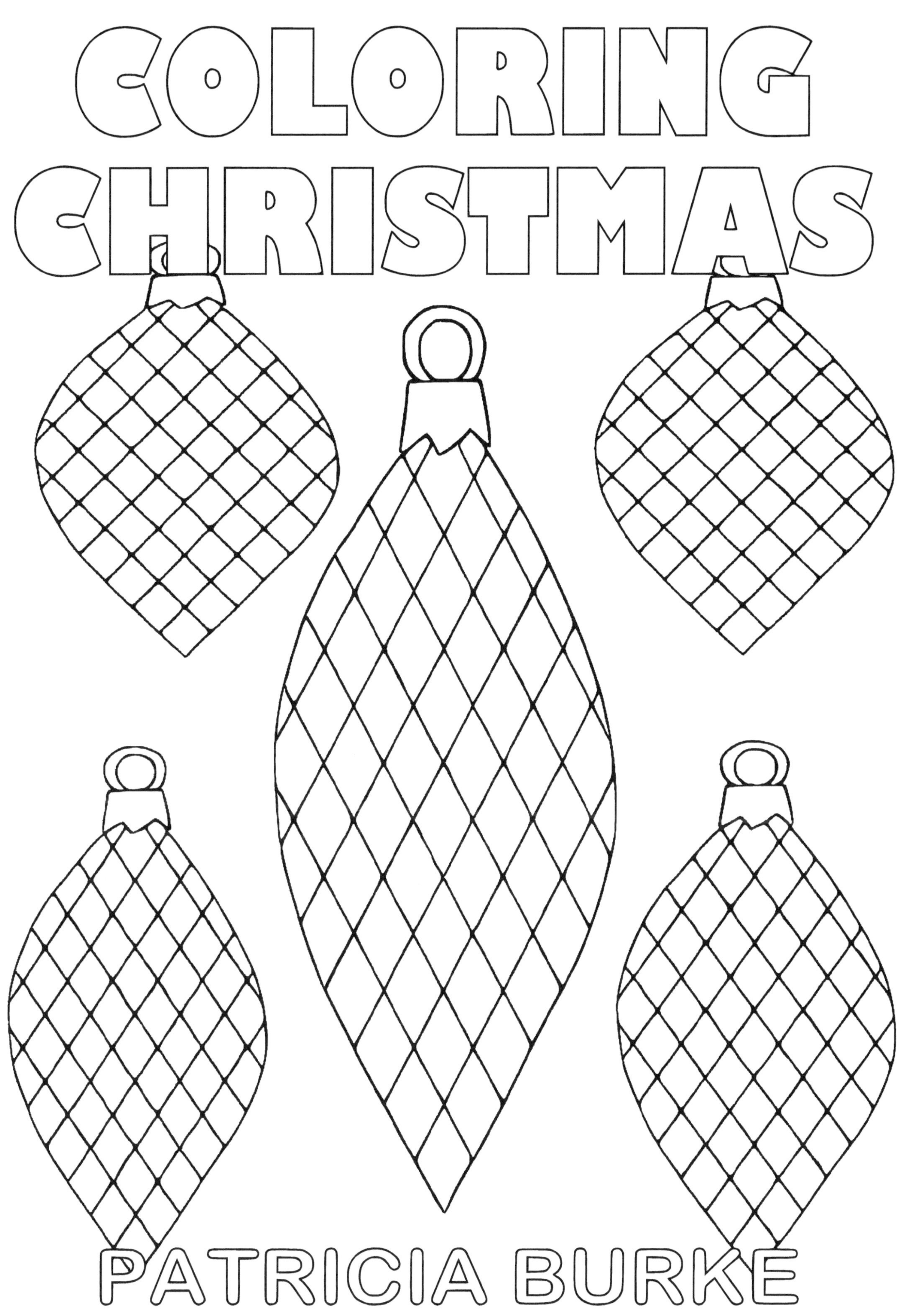
COLORING CHRISTMAS
PATRICIA BURKE

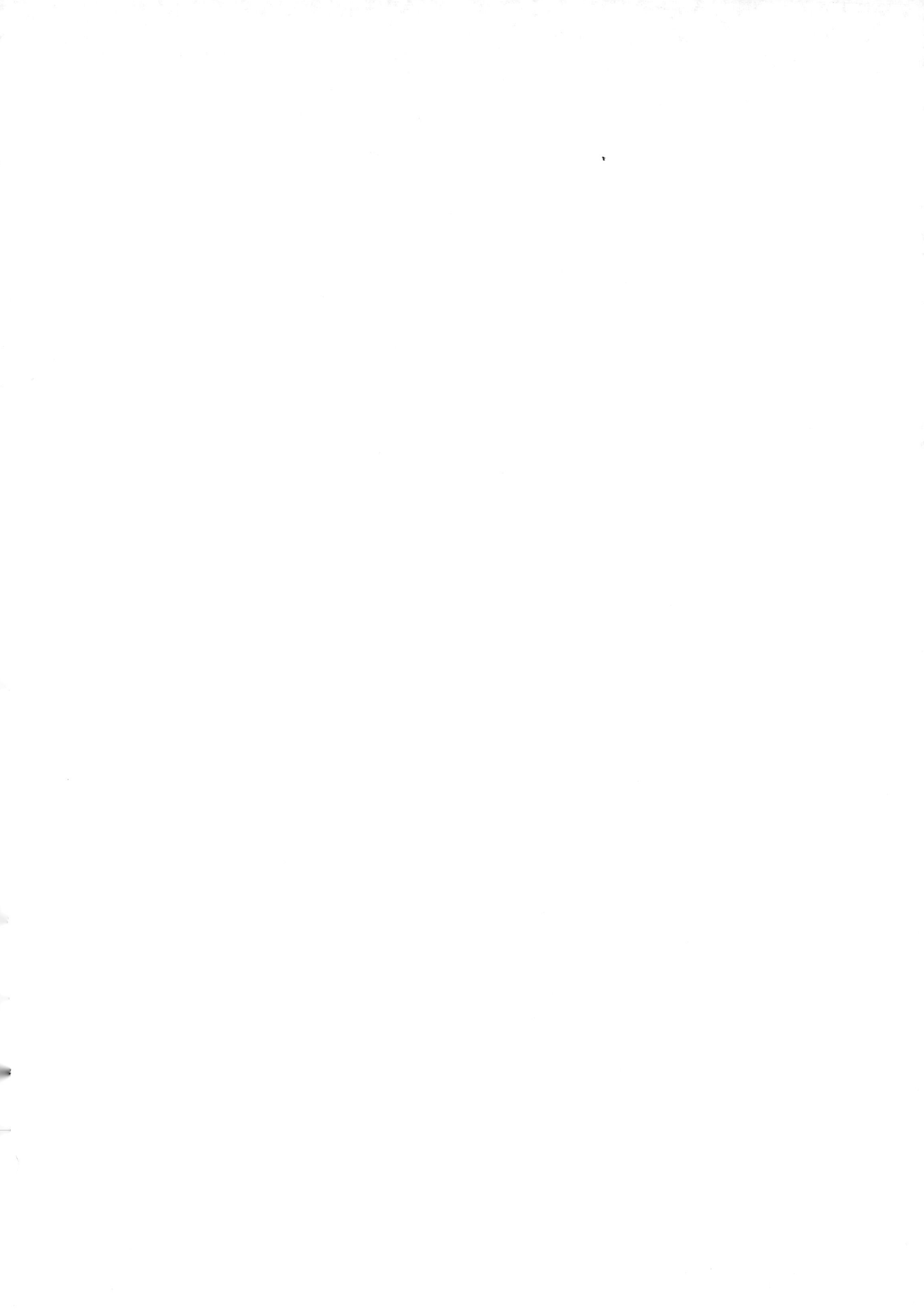

www.ingramcontent.com/pod-product-compliance
Lightning Source LLC
LaVergne TN
LVHW080926110826
845155LV00039B/221

* 9 7 8 1 9 5 1 5 7 6 0 5 9 *